EELS

SEA MONSTERS

HOMER SEWARD

The Rourke Press, Inc.
Vero Beach, Florida 32964

9901052

PHOTO CREDITS
All photos © Marty Snyderman except © James Rowan: page 6 ;
© Lynn M. Stone: page 13

EDITORIAL SERVICES:
Penworthy Learning Systems

Library of Congress Cataloging-in-Publication Data

Seward, Homer. 1942-
   Eels / by Homer Seward.
     p. cm. — (Sea monsters)
   Includes index
   Summary: Introduces eels, their physical appearance, types, where they
live, their habits, predators and prey.
   ISBN 1-57103-235-5
   1. Eels—Juvenile literature. [1. Eels.] I. Title.
II. Series: Seward, Homer, 1942-   Sea monsters.
QL637.9.A5S48 1998
597'.43—dc21   98–24061
                                                 CIP
                                                 AC

Printed in the USA

TABLE OF CONTENTS

Eels 5

Eels as Sea Monsters 6

What Eels Look Like 8

Where Eels Live 11

Habits of Eels 12

Predator and Prey 14

Kinds of Eels 17

Eels and People 18

The Eels That Aren't 20

Glossary 23

Index 24

EELS

They're long, slim, slimy, and wiggly. They look a lot like snakes, but they're not snakes. They're eels, and they're fish.

Eels look quite frightening. Many of them have jaws full of sharp teeth.

Most **species** (SPEE sheez), or kinds, of eels are small. The biggest eels, though, are about 10 feet (3 meters) long. If the biggest eels could grab a basketball rim in their jaws, their tails would swish on the floor.

A colorful moray eel bares its teeth to warn an undersea photographer.

EELS AS SEA MONSTERS

Oceans aren't really homes for monsters. But they are homes for some rather frightening and dangerous animals. These are the kinds of animals people sometimes *call* monsters.

The speckled moray has sharp teeth and a quick temper.

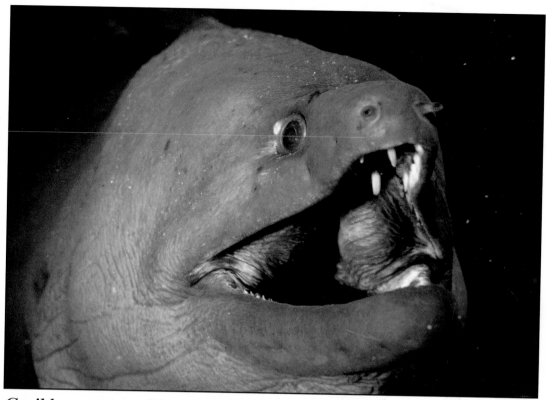

Caribbean moray, like others in its family, is best left alone.

Eels can bite. A large moray eel's bite can crush bones.

Some eels have a poisonous bite. Some have poisonous flesh. An electric eel can shock anyone who handles it. Yes, eels not only look scary, they can hurt a person.

7

WHAT EELS LOOK LIKE

Eels come in many sizes and colors. The largest, one of the morays, weighs over 100 pounds (45 kilograms). Some of the conger eels are nearly as large as the 10-foot (3-meter) morays.

Eels may be silvery, brown, greenish, or a mix of colors and spots. Most eels are shaped like round sticks. Some species, however, have long, flat bodies, like canoe paddles.

Nearly all fish have scales. But most eels have smooth skin without scales.

The ribbon eel of the South Pacific relies on camouflage rather than its jaws for its survival.

WHERE EELS LIVE

Most eels live in warm waters. Some eels travel from the oceans into rivers and streams. In the United States, the American eel lives part of its life in freshwater streams in the East.

Most species of eels live in shallow seas. A few, however, live in seas one mile (1,609 meters) deep.

Divers often find eels in rocky places, on reefs, and in sunken ships.

Eels like to tuck themselves away between rocks or coral formations.

HABITS OF EELS

Most eels are **nocturnal** (nahk TER nul). They are more active at night than by day. During the day, many eels hide between rocks or in other dark places.

A spotted snake eel hides itself in sand and waits for prey to swim by.

After a dive, a cormorant surfaces with a small eel snack.

Several eels **migrate** (MY grayt). That means they travel long distances at certain times of the year. The American eel, for example, migrates from fresh water to the sea.

13

PREDATOR AND PREY

Most eels are **predators** (PRED uh turz). They catch and eat many different kinds of animals that live in the water. Conger eels, for example, eat other fish, crabs, lobsters, and octopuses. The animals the eels catch are their **prey** (PRAY).

The little garden eel eats tiny animals that drift through the sea. Some of a garden eel's prey are too small for us to see.

Eels, in turn, are prey for predators larger than themselves. Sea birds often catch eels.

Sharp teeth show that many eels are predators of other marine animals.

KINDS OF EELS

Many kinds of eels live in the oceans along the coasts of North America. The American eel is the only species found in fresh water in North America.

Scientists know of 450 species of eels in at least 20 families, or groups. Sixteen species worldwide are freshwater eels.

Among the most interesting of all eels—and all fish—are the electric eels. Their bodies create an electric charge to jolt their enemies and to kill prey.

Scientists know some 80 kinds of moray eels, including this Caribbean moray being cleaned by gobies.

EELS AND PEOPLE

People have different feelings about eels. Many people don't like eels because they are slimy and squiggly. And most people aren't fond of being shocked or bitten.

Diver feeds a hungry moray.

With food, a diver tempts an eel from its hiding place.

Eels are prized in some parts of the world for their flesh. Even in the United States, many people find eels a tasty seafood.

In Rome, fish farmers began raising eels for food at least 2,100 years ago.

THE EELS THAT AREN'T

Spiny eels are a group of fish that live in deep ocean water. They have an eel shape, but they are not eels.

Lampreys (LAM prayz), often called lamprey eels, have long, snaky bodies. But lampreys are not eels.

Lampreys don't have jaws. They have mouths and sharp teeth, but their mouths are like suction cups. Several kinds of lampreys use their teeth to attach themselves to other fish. They suck the fish's flesh, slowly killing the fish.

Like many fish called "eel," the wolf eel is not considered a true eel by marine scientists.

GLOSSARY

migrate (MY grayt) — to travel to a distant place at the same time each year, often in groups

nocturnal (nahk TER nul) — active at night rather than by day

predator (PRED uh tur) — an animal that hunts other animals for food

prey (PRAY) — an animal that is hunted by another animal for food

species (SPEE sheez) — within a group of closely related animals, one certain kind, such as an *American* eel

Shrimp surround a moray eel tucked in its hiding place.

INDEX

colors   8

divers   11

eels   5, 7, 8, 11, 12, 13,
14, 17, 18
  American   13, 17
  conger   8, 14
  electric   7, 17
  freshwater   17
  garden   14
  moray   7, 8
  spiny   20

fish   5, 8, 14, 20

lampreys   20

people   18

predators   14

prey   14

scales   8

species   17

teeth   5, 20

United States   11, 19

FURTHER READING

Find out more about eels with these helpful books:
Ling, Mary. *Amazing Fish.* Knopf, 1991.
Taylor, David. *Animal Monsters.* Lerner, 1989.